The Very Hungover Caterpillar

CONSTABLE

First published in Great Britain in 2014 by Constable

Copyright in text © 2014 Josie Lloyd and Emlyn Rees
Copyright in illustrations © 2014 Gillian Johnson

7 9 10 8 6

The moral right of the authors has been asserted.

A CIP catalogue record for this book
is available from the British Library.

ISBN 978-1-47211-710-6

Page design by Design23
Printed and bound in Italy by L.E.G.O. SpA

Constable
An imprint of
Little, Brown Book Group
Carmelite House
50 Victoria Embankment
London EC4Y 0DZ

An Hachette UK Company
www.hachette.co.uk

www.littlebrown.co.uk

THE VERY
HUNGOVER
CATERPILLAR
A Parody

Josie Lloyd & Emlyn Rees
Illustrated by Gillian Johnson

CONSTABLE • LONDON

In the gloom of the room, a fully dressed man lies on the sofa.

The next morning,
the TV comes on and – ugh! –

up lurches a thirsty and very
hungover caterpillar.

He starts to look for a cure.

At 7 a.m., he has one paracetamol –
but he is still hungover.

At 8 a.m., he has two cups of sweet tea and calls in sick — but he is still hungover.

At 9 a.m., he has three slices of toast, two fizzy vitamin pills and a black coffee –

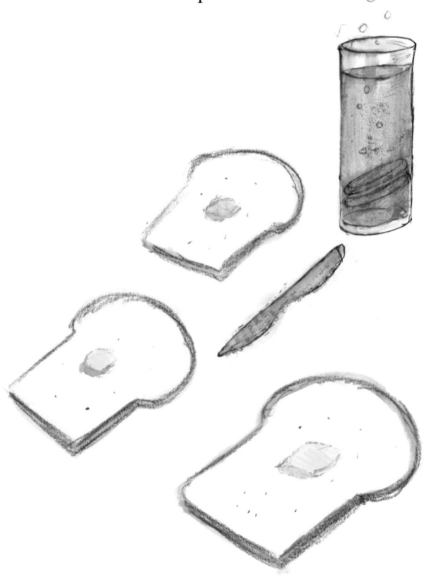

but he is still hungover.

At 11 a.m., he has four rashers of bacon, three sausages, two eggs and a slice of fried bread –

but he is still hungover.

By 4 p.m., he has watched
five hours of daytime TV,
ignored four text messages,

eaten three family-sized packets of Hula Hoops,
two Pot Noodles

and has drunk a litre bottle of full fat coke —
but he is still hungover.

At 8 p.m., he orders one chicken tikka masala, one lamb biryani, one pilau rice …

… one tarka dhal, one aloo gobi, one onion bhaji, one naan, one chapatti, and washes it all down with one tub of double choc-chip ice-cream – but he is still hungover.

After that, he has a massive tummyache.

Now he isn't just a hungover caterpillar anymore. He is a bloated, smelly hungover caterpillar.

He guzzles one big green bottle of indigestion
medicine, does a huge burp, and
feels slightly better.

He has a shave and a shower and cocoons
himself inside his duvet.

He stays inside for more than twelve hours.

Then he stretches, pushes his way out,
and finally . . .

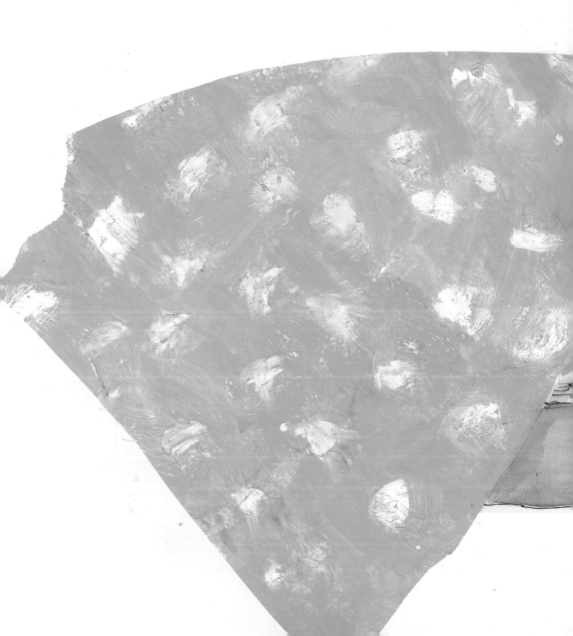

he floats

like a

butterfly!